Post Like An INFLUENCER, Grow Like A MARKETER

Justin Monsanto

Want me to personally mentor you in the art of social media?

This book is going to personally show you how to post better content and grow your fanbase on Instagram.

If you follow these steps, I can almost guarantee that you WILL be getting hundreds; if not thousands of followers and engagement weekly. But that depends on the amount of work you are willing to put in.

In fact, I'm so sure of this process that I'll throw in a free cheat sheet of this process. Instead of having to go through this whole book again, you can easily find different parts if you have trouble.

But social media is a crazy world. Algorithms change and update rapidly. What do you do when one part of the plan does not work anymore?

Well, I've thought about that ahead of time. I have an email list of present and future social media masters like yourself.

Once you're on my list, I'll send out monthly emails updating you on the latest changes on each of the major social media platforms (Facebook, Instagram, Twitter, etc.) You'll get nothing less than helpful advice and won't be spammed.

Interested?

Go to
**https://mailchi.mp/74d02e4344d5/
master-social-media**
get the FREE MASTERING
INSTAGRAM cheat sheet, and join
my mailing list now.

CONTENTS

CHAPTER 1:
IMAGINE YOURSELF AS AN INFLUENCER WITH THOUSANDS OF FANS WHO LOVE YOUR WORK.

What if you could wake up in the morning, check your phone, and <u>BAM!</u> You notice it's been blowing up all night. That photo you posted right before going to bed got <u>THOUSANDS</u> of likes and <u>HUNDREDS</u> of comments.

You scan through the comments and see a sea of people who love the photo, many people put heart emoji's on every photo you post, and the occasional hate messages (hey, you know you poppin when you have haters).

Now, what if I told you that photo was a promotion for a small sunglasses business. A brand that paid <u>YOU</u> to post a photo of <u>THEIR</u> products?

You quickly check your bank account and notice that there's a deposit of $300 in your account. Essentially you made $300 in your sleep.

What if this wasn't just a one-time thing? If you could do this week in and week out. Getting paid AND gifts from people and brands in exchange for promotion.

What if you got so many message requests that your DM's are full. You have to become picky about who you choose to promote, so you don't lose your followers.

Sounds too good to be true?

Well, It's Not

There are numerous people from celebrities to stay at home parents who are growing a following and making money through Instagram.

Regular people like you and me.

Doctors

Lawyers

Video Game Lovers (Like me)

That annoying kid who never stops taking selfies

I want to add your name and your passion to this list.

I want you to imagine growing a following on Instagram that loves YOU.

I want you to imagine getting hundreds of new followers each week, with thousands of new followers each month.

I want you to imagine being able to get paid in hundreds and even thousands of dollars from people and brands for promotions. Even drive your audience to your own business or other content.

It doesn't matter if your current Instagram account doesn't have the growth that you want. It doesn't even matter if you NEVER had an Instagram account before.

Because I'm going to walk with you step-by-step on how to start your Instagram in the right way. How to grow your following of rabid, engagement loving following that is passionate about the same things you.

All you need to do is <u>BELIEVE</u>! Have the confidence, desire, and motivation to make this happen no matter what.

Because once you get your mindset right, the action becomes second nature.

So I want you to imagine having thousands of followers and making money off Instagram.

What would your life look like?

How would it feel having 10,000 followers and making an extra $1,000 per month?

What would you do with all this money and influence?

Promote your Twitch or YouTube channel to your audience of loving followers?

Convert your followers into customers or clients for your business?

Use the platform to become a voice or expert in a specific field?

Trust me, having influence is amazing.

What if you got so big that your followers wanted more?

What if you were making enough money that you could quit your job?

Now you have time to put out more content.

This is possible.

I promise you that all of this is possible and I will show you the strategy that influencers and social media managers implement later in this book.

No more bosses

No daily rush to get to work

You get to do the things that YOU love to do.

But it won't be easy.

Like all good things, it takes time and patience. I do not promise you that you can quit your job tomorrow and instantly make an extra $1,000/month next week.

I promise you that if you're patient and you follow the plan consistently, you are going to live the life you've been dreaming of.

Are you ready?

CHAPTER 2: BEFORE YOU EVEN GET STARTED ON THIS JOURNEY.

I feel like this part is so important that we need to discuss it twice before getting to it.

This is NOT a make money quick strategy. This is NOT an overnight success strategy.

Any overnight success you've seen comes from work that you don't see (unless you go on a daytime talk show and say a catchy, meme-worthy catchphrase)

When you first start out on this journey, there will be a lot of research.

What kind of Instagram page do you make? What content do you post? What hashtags do you use to get the most exposure?

This is the same thing I had to do (and am still doing) to grow my gaming Instagram page.

At the end of each chapter, there will be a series of action steps. Don't worry about following these steps if you're reading this book for the first time.

Read through the entire book, get a feel for the process, then read the book a second time while performing the action steps.

That way you know exactly what you are getting into and are ready to take action.

Who is This Guy Giving Me Advice?

First, let me introduce myself. My name is Justin, and for the longest of time, I really didn't care about social media.

If you ever come across any of my personal social media pages, I never made an effort in growing them or my influence.

I wanted to learn more about how social media worked after I tried starting a career as a content creator and as a drop shipper on Shopify.

I started creating content on YouTube when I was 19. I bought a Canon Rebel T3I camera from my local pawn shop, bought some cheap lights and a green screen that I never used, and began to record.

My first channel was called JustTalks. It was really a variety show because I never had a focus on the kind of content I wanted to make.

I started getting into a groove when I was posting news stories on my channel. Whenever a breaking story showed on the news, I quickly turned on my camera and began recording. I wanted to be first on the scene.

The most views I ever got on a video was around 2,000. But my interest in news faded with time, and I just decided to give up on the whole channel.

After working several years as a delivery biker for Postmates and Grubhub, I searched the internet trying to find a way to build an online business. My research brought me to an Ad from a guy named Alex Becker.

If you don't know who Alex Becker is, just Google his name once. I'm pretty sure you'll be bombarded with Ads 5 minutes later.

He and another guy named Justin Cener teamed up to offer a drop shipping course where they taught you how to sell items from your own Shopify store, use the money to buy the item from a Chinese wholesaler for nickels on the dollar, then keep the difference as profit. I paid $1,000 for that course thinking it'd be my way to good life.

My first store was this barebones elephant themed store that sold jewelry.
I created the store, targeted my audience down to the most rabid elephant loving people in the United States.

I began writing blogs about elephants and promoting those blogs using Facebook Ads.

Those blogs gained a lot of traction early on, thousands of likes and reactions, hundreds of comments, and people were visiting my website.

(Insert Elephant Pals Photo here)

The problem was that no one was buying.

I was losing money on these Facebook Ads and needed to come up with a way to start making sales fast.

While learning the business, I also got to learn about influencer marketing. Getting social media pages with big followings to promote your products to their followers.

I found an elephant page and emailed the owner. He charged me $50 for 2 posts (which I realize now was a steal) that stood on his page for three days each.

Traffic increased dramatically, and people were buying left and right. All because of these two posts.

Eventually, I had to let go of the Shopify dream after the elephant store and gaming store I opened both failed. These were due to numerous problems from not having the money to keep the store up, and the warehouses not having the products I needed.

But the thought of two Instagram posts boosting my sales caught my attention. So I spent the next two years studying what makes these Instagram profiles so influential that they can tell their followers where to buy.

That's when I learned the strategies that we'll go through.

Strategies that social media managers charge hundreds of dollars <u>PER HOUR</u> to perform and Influencers use to grow their brands.

How to build an Instagram account from the ground up that focuses on <u>YOUR</u> passion.

How to efficiently create and curate great content that draws in a niche audience that loves your passion as much as you do.

How to monetize your successful Instagram account through paid shoutouts and even draw your followers to your own business.

Enough sizzle, let's get to this steak.

CHAPTER 3:
WHAT'S YOUR PASSION AND WHO ARE YOU TRYING TO ATTRACT?

Do you want to know why I failed so much previously?

Was it because I was young? No

Was it because of lack of money or information? Maybe.

Was it because I didn't love what I was doing?

Absolutely!

If you don't love the content that you're posting on Instagram, you'll be bored and eventually quit.

I'm not going to let you make the same mistake that I made.

In this section, I'm going to walk with you through the process of discovering what you're truly passionate about.

You'll also learn how to use this to find the niche audience that has the same passion as you.

What Type of Page Are You?

You know those quizzes on Facebook that tells you what TV show character you are? What Game of Thrones character are you? What Family Guy character are you?

We're going to do something like that with Instagram. We are going to find out what account you should be.

Every Instagram account can generally fall into one of three categories.

Personal Page

Business Page

Repost Page

The page you belong in really depends on what content you'll be posting and what your end game on Instagram is about.

Let's discuss each page further and see what type of person matches with them.

Personal Pages

Personal pages are...well personal. They're used to highlight the person who owns the account. Almost everyone you follow on Instagram has a personal page.

They take selfies.

They take pictures while visiting cool places.

They eat some good food.

They cuddle with their pets.

Everything is about...well them.
What people who have personal pages do is focus on their PERSONAL BRAND.

In my opinion, personal pages are the most flexible Instagram pages you can have.

You can post pretty much anything you want.

From Travel photos

Food Pictures

Funny videos

Even random selfies throughout the day.

There's just one rule to personal pages. You <u>NEED</u> to be in every picture.

People follow personal pages for the person.

Have you ever seen these Instagram pages for people's cats and dogs?

You know why they're so popular? Because it's all about the cat or the dog. No one cares about the scratching post or the dog food they're having that day.

The same goes for people.

You need to be the main focus of every post.

Going on vacation? Have someone take a photo of you on the beach.

Eating a great lunch? Take a selfie of you taking a bite out of your food.

Taking random selfies? Get those angles right and take it.

You are the highlight of your personal page.

If you don't like taking photos of yourself at all. Then the next two sections will definitely work for you.

Business Pages

Business pages are similar to personal pages, except that they focus solely on the business.

Everything from the people who work on the business down to the products they serve.

Followers want to know what you are offering to them?

When are you open?

What specials do you have?

Having a social media presence can do wonders for your business.

Take for example The Sweetshop NYC.

I used to work weekends then one summer. No better way to spend a summer vacation than scooping ice cream for impatient New Yorkers on a 90-degree day.

The one thing I admired about the shop, and Kelly who owns it, was the way they handled Instagram.

Kelly would take photos of any new flavors we'd get in the shop.

Take a photo of the ice cream and candy menu, so our customers knew what we had.

He even leveraged any celebrations going on.

During the PRIDE parade. Kelly posted a picture of our rainbow snowball. Which was a snow cone with watermelon, green apple, blue raspberry, and lemon (if I remembered this correctly)?

All he did was caption it with the hashtag #Loveislove

An hour later we had a line down the block from people who came from the parade in the Village to the Upper East Side.

For those of you who haven't been to New York City, that's quite a trip.
If you plan on utilizing Instagram to draw people to your business or website, this is the kind of account you should be focusing on.

It's the type of account I focused on for my gaming page BagMannTV (check me out here).

If you're too nervous to take photos of yourself and don't have a business to promote, or don't even want to create your own content.

There's an Instagram Account for you.

Repost Pages

If you want to post some of the most viral content surrounding your passion. A repost page is definitely for you.

Repost pages and hands down are the easiest pages to post content and grow. Because you are not creating any of the content.

Instead, you are reposting viral content in your passion and niche.

I guess I can call it the drop shipping of Instagram.

Multiple niche profiles have this kind of account.

Travel

Entrepreneurship

Quotes

Luxury

Art

Celebrities

I can keep going on and on with this list.

But to me, Repost accounts are one of the most annoying.

Not only are you constrained to the specific niche you chose but you also have to do more research to find content that will go viral.

If you know you want to curate or use other people's content.

If you're looking for the account type with the fastest growth rate on Instagram

Reposting accounts are where you want to be.

Passion = Content

I want you to keep this equation in your head from now on.

Passion = Content

As long as you have a passion for something, you'll always have content.

But then the question becomes "what is my passion."

Many of us love different things.

Sports

Knitting

Finances

Dungeons and Dragons

How are we supposed to choose which passion to base our Instagram account off?

Here's how.

List all of the things that you are passionate about.

Just make a large list of everything that you like from working out all the way down to those doughnuts you had after "working out."

After you write between 10-20 passions that you have, look at your list and ask yourself.

"Which one of these can I talk about for hours without being bored."

Slowly cross some of those things out.

Dungeons and Dragons? Never played it before (but always wanted to).

Knitting? Outside of knit one purl two, I'm clueless.

Just keep crossing things off your list until you reach the number one thing you can talk forever about.

Congratulations, we just found your niche.

Chances are, you are already an expert in it too.

You know and can talk about more topics in this niche than most people.

For instance, take my passion.

For my account, I chose video games.

I consider myself an expert in this passion because I can talk forever about different issues in this industry.

You want to have a debate on Whether Battlefield or Call of Duty is a better First Person Shooter? I'm in.

You want to talk about whether Starcraft has better tournaments than Dota 2? Okay.

You want to debate whether PC is better than Playstation and Xbox… Well, I'm not going to debate that because those get ugly quick.

Here's a great way to test if you really found your passion.

Go to meetup.com

They literally have tons of free and low-cost event for people of all types of passions.

The best part is that everyone in a meetup group are extremely passionate people.

Find around 3-5 meetup groups in your chosen niche and start going to events.

Don't just go to one event and decide you don't want to do this passion because you didn't talk to anyone.

I was scared when I went to my first meetup event; it was a Sign Language meetup group that I had to attend for a language course in college.

It takes at least two meetings before you get comfortable enough to dive in. Once you do, start talking and getting to know the people at these events.

Learn what they love about your passion, what they hate about it.

Towards the end of the event, ask if they have Instagram so you can follow. You just found some potential followers for your account.

What Does Your Audience Like on Instagram?

Okay, so you found your main passion.

Went to a few meetup events and found some people who may follow you. We must be ready to start making this page right?

Not just yet.

We may have found our passion and our audience.

But we don't know what they like. What content they comment on.

But we will do that right now.

It's time to do some investigating through Instagram.

The great thing about Instagram is that you are just one search away from seeing all the content people like.

Go on Instagram and click on the magnifying glass on the bottom of the app (or the search bar if you're on pc).

Type in some simple hashtag in the search bar.

#Gaming, #gamerlife, and #videogames would be mine.

Once you click search, you see tons of different photos.

See if there is a pattern for all of the hashtags or if different content is popular when you search different ones.

Write down a list of content that has at least 300 likes and at least 20 comments.

Keep this list handy for when we start creating content.

Who Is My Audience Following?

Do you know who the top influencers are in your niche?

Well, it's time to find out.

Go to Google.

Type "Top ten *enter passion here* influencers to follow on Instagram."

You should be able to find at least one list that has the top influencers in your niche.

Write down these names and keep that list closeby.

These will be the first people you follow when you create your Instagram account.

Check out their profile, their content, and their following.

Are they posting the same content that we researched? Is it popular on their page? Are their followers engaging in their posts? Both likes and comments?

Some of the top influencers I see in the gaming niche are.

Ninja

PewDiePie

TmarTn

These are some of the top gamers that I watch on YouTube and Twitch.

If you keep following the steps, some of their followers will discover and start following you.

Action Steps

1) Choose the type of account you want to create (Personal, Business, Repost)
2) Discover what is your greatest passion, and who is your niche audience.
    a) Bonus: Attend Meetup events to test your passion and meet potential followers
3) Discover the types of content that is popular among your niche audience
4) Find the top influencers in your passion and niche. Look at their profile, content, and followers.

CHAPTER 4: LAYING THE FOUNDATION FOR YOUR INSTAGRAM ACCOUNT.

Okay, we finally finished our research.

We found our passion, we found our niche audience, and we found the content they like.

It's time to create our Instagram account and give the people what they want.

In this chapter, I'm going to show you how to lay the foundation for a successful Instagram Page. We're going to go over picking the perfect profile name and picture that draws people into your profile. Writing the perfect bio to get them know a bit about you, and want to know more.

Finally, how to utilize the website space to convert our followers into an audience, customers, or clients.

Choosing the PERFECT Instagram Name and Profile Picture to Draw Visitors to Your Page.

Josh Altman

Ninja

Nike

You know what these three have in common?

These are short, easy to remember names which a lot of people know. They also have a little under 81 million followers between them.

You want to be there too right? Then your name on Instagram has to catch people's attention and be memorable.

But what name do you pick?

The answer is really easy.

It depends on the type of account that you have as well as the content you'll be posting.

Having a personal, business, or repost page makes all the difference of what your name should be.

If you decide to go in with the personal page, your Instagram name would actually be YOUR NAME.

But there's some difficulty that comes with this. If you have a "common name" that can easily belong to a lot of people, it'll take a little creativity to get your name.

For instance, let's use John Doe.
Pretty common name right?

Even people who aren't yet identified are known as John (or Jane) Doe.

So it's going to be hard to get names like @JohnDoe, @John.Doe, or even @John_Doe

The best thing you can do is put a number after your name. Make it meaningful so that people can associate you with that number.

If you played sports and your number was 14, you can be @JohnDoe14.

But @JohnDoe12345 doesn't look too good, so keep your numbers to not more than 2 digits.

If you don't want numbers in your name, you can put the word "The" or add your profession either before your name or after.

@TheJoshAltman

@WWERollins

These kinds of names put you in the forefront of people's minds because you are being known as "The" guy or establishing the profession that you are in.

The last thing you want to do is play around with the capitalization of letters or switching them out for symbols.

It just doesn't look professional.

Pick which Instagram handle would you not trust.

@JohnDoe14 @TheJohnDoe, @JohnDoeWWE or @joHndoE

If you are going to be creating a business page, the Name HAS to be the name of the business.

This is just a Business 101 lesson, but make sure you do have a catchy name that shows what your business does and memorable to potential customers or clients.

@TheSweetshopNYC

@Risingdragontattoos

@Glossier

They each have something that is memorable to people who find them, and also shows a bit about what their business does.

If by some twist of luck that your business' name isn't available, go further about what your business does.

If @Glossier were taken, I'd change it to @GlossierSkin because their tagline reads "Skin first, makeup second."

Repost pages are a little interesting.

You have to be more creative with the name because the chances are <u>MANY</u> that other pages have taken the names you're thinking of.

You want to create a repost page about luxury living? Don't try to call it @Luxury, it's already taken and has over 1 million followers.

But you can Niche it down further to a specific luxury item. Give yourself a name like @Luxuryliving @LuxuryHouses @Luxuryboats.

Playing around with the name while still staying with what your page is about is a great way to name a repost page.

Since I'm creating a business page for my real estate business.

Just keep the name simple, catchy, and related to your content and you'll attract people.

Just like your Instagram name, your profile picture also needs to catch people's attention.

Many people will notice your profile picture before noticing your name. With the low attention span many people have now, that profile picture better gets their attention quick.

The tips for choosing the right name can be used for selecting the right profile picture.

If you have a personal account, the profile picture has to be of you. Take some selfies or grab some friends and do a photoshoot together. Make it fun so that the joy can be reflected in the picture.

The only additional rule is to make sure your profile picture only shows YOU.

We all love our friends, but you don't want someone who follows your page thinking it was your friends Instagram.

Business profiles have one specific rule.

Your profile picture SHOULD BE the logo of your business.

I say should be because I know a lot of businesses that consist of one person performing a service.

Lawyers

Accountants

Dentists

If you fit among this group, do a hybrid of business and personal strategies for your page.

For the other businesses it has to be the logo.

You want people to remember who you are? Well, more people will remember an image than a name. When was the last time you heard someone say "I know the name of the place, but I don't how the logo looked"?

Rarely, if ever. Most of the time it's the other way around.

I'm not going to hold a marketing lecture on how to create a great logo for your business. But I will refer you to some websites if you don't have a logo yet.

1) Fiverr.com: They literally have freelancers who will do almost anything for $5. I've had all my logos done this way, and I've been nothing less than satisfied with them.
2) Upwork.com: If the low cost of Fiverr makes you think you'll have low quality work, go with Upwork. They have a large network of Freelancers as well. They also allow you to post a job and have Freelancers bid to take it. So you can get great work at a bargain.
3) Canva.com: If you're creative (or have no budget) and decided to make your own logo, Canva is the perfect place. They have tons of different sizes, fonts, images to make your logo stand out. I don't do this because graphic design is FAR from my specialty.

If you decide to make your own logo or hire someone to do it, make sure you know the dimensions of Instagrams profile picture. As of the time of me writing this book, the current dimensions are 110 x 110. But a quick Google search will tell you everything. This is very important or else you'll have a logo that is cut off.

A repost page has some options in what profile picture to choose. You can either create a logo for your page or choose an image that reflects your content.

If you're going with the luxury cars niche from earlier, you can create a logo around your page's name (like LC for luxury cars) or have a photo of a luxury car. Just make sure it's good enough to catch the eye.

Creating The Perfect Bio That Turns Visitors Into Followers.

So you came up with the perfect name and have a great profile picture. Awesome, you'll definitely get visitors to click on your page. Now it's time to attack this bio.

It pains me when people opt not to write <u>ANYTHING</u> in their bio.

Yes, the photos and videos on your page are important. We'll tackle that in another chapter. But before people see your content, they will see your bio.

It's a great place to turn visitors into followers.

There are three rules to a good bio.

1) K.I.S.S.
2) Create a hashtag for your content.
3) Use related emoji's to make your bio pop and point to link.

I'm pretty sure you already know what K.I.S.S. stands for.

If not, let me be the first to tell you.

Keep
It
Simple
Stupic

I've been preaching simplicity for a lot of these tips so far.

That's because simpler means it's easier to read.

You want people to visit your page to read your bio?

So keep it simple by following these three basics.

1) Explain what you do
2) Where you're from
3) What you offer

Here's an example of a good starting bio

Mixer & Twitch Streamer. Can change faces with a change of a bag. Join the Baggie Army Thursday-Monday.

You can twist this method in a variety of ways to fit your page.

Once you have the text, you have the identity of your profile.

But that identity looks a little boring just leaving text there.

Now we're going to dress up your bio.

One of the best ways to dress up your bio is to add RELATABLE emoji's. A few well thought of emoji will add an extra pop to your bio.

Don't put a smiling poop emoji unless you are a plumber.

You can put a computer emoji if you're a gamer like my example. You can have cars if you're doing a luxury car page. There's pretty much an emoji for anything.

One of the newest features Instagram has added is the ability to follow hashtags.

While we're going to dive into hashtags pretty soon, it's important to know about this feature as it can affect the way people find content.

Even if someone follows you on Instagram, Instagram may not show them all of the content you upload if the algorithm thinks they don't like it.

Instead of following specific people to find their content, users can now follow specific hashtags and see content that has that hashtag.

You can take advantage of this by coming up with your own hashtag and post that in your bio while telling visitors to go follow it. Now you have two ways of showing your content to users. First through your profile, and through the hashtag.

Use these three methods, and you have the makings of a great bio to capture new followers.

Adding Your Website to Drive Viewers Wherever You Want Them to.

If you were writing out your bio, you would probably have seen a small box that says "website" on it. This is the one box you must <u>ABSOLUTELY</u> put something in.

Instagram is strict when it comes to links that take users out of their platform. If you try to put a link in the description of any photo or video you post, anyone who sees it will not be able to click on the link or copy it.

And no, a majority of people will not go to their internet browser and manually type in a link that they saw on a post. It does not matter how much they may love you.

Instagram does allow you to have this one area in your profile where you can post a link that anyone can click on.

Many of you who are reading this probably have another platform outside of Instagram.

I've met business owners, YouTubers, Twitch Broadcasters, Musicians who have all used Instagram as a tool for gaining followings. Then they would take those followers and drive them to their other platforms using their website section.

You need to do the same thing.

Whether it's your personal blog, a podcast, YouTube channel. Shopify store, or anything else. Put a link to it in your website section.

If you have a huge, confusing URL like the ones YouTube gives creators who are just starting out. Use a URL shortener website to make it a little more pleasing. Google, YouTube, Amazon, and Bitly.com all have URL shortening tools that can help you out.

If you do use these, it's best to let your followers know what the link goes to in your bio. You can even have hand emoji's that points down towards the URL, so it entices people to click on it.

There's one more thing about websites that you should NEVER do as a courtesy to others.

Do Not Spam Your Link To Everyone

You will not believe how many people DM me or comment on my page asking me to follow them on Twitch, to subscribe to their YouTube channel, to do anything like a "return" for following me.

No one owes you anything, and it is just annoying to spam your channel and profiles when I haven't even gotten the chance to know anything about you or your content. If you provide enough value to others, they will click on your link under their own free will.

You just learned how to lay the foundation for an amazing profile.

Now it's time to dive into the most fun part of Instagram, which is your content.

ACTION STEPS

1) Choose a great name and profile picture that shows who you are and what your profile is about.

2) Write a short bio that describes you and your profile to turn visitors into followers.

    a) Bonus: Add some hand emojis pointing down towards your URL,

3) Have a website and ONLY put it in the website section of your profile.

CHAPTER 5: TO CREATE MY OWN CONTENT, OR STEAL FROM SOMEONE ELSE.

You identified your passion and audience. You laid the best foundation for success on your Instagram Account.

Now it is time to focus on the most important part of social media...the content.

Remember this one important phrase; content is king.

Everything you've already done and everything you are going to do next will not make a difference if you do not post good, consistent content.

In this chapter, you will learn how to plan and organize your content as a Social Media Manager. You will also learn to create and curate content like an influencer.

If you can master this aspect of Instagram, then everything else will be easy.

How to Research and Organize Content Like a Social Media Manager.

You know what's the biggest problem an influencer will face online? Running out of content to post.

This was a problem that I faced a lot. I'd get in a groove, posting a lot of pictures over the span of a few days. Then I'd be completely out of ideas.

I learned a solution to this problem when I worked as a film and social media intern for Life Vest Inside.

One of my responsibilities was to curate content to post on their Facebook, Instagram, and Twitter accounts.

That's when they introduced me to content calendars.

They created a list of content that they planned to post. This list had over a month worth of posts on it. Complete with image, description, and hashtags.

I was amazed to see such a thing. I never even thought about creating one of these for my accounts.

But how do we create a content calendar?

The easy way of doing it is to open up a new spreadsheet on either Excel or Google Sheets.

On the first row, you'll name each category like so.

a) Posting Date
b) Image
c) Description
d) Hashtags

If you don't want to create your own content calendar. You can also download the app Buffer. The buffer is a content management app that lets you schedule posts and descriptions ahead of time.

But there is a warning; Buffer will not actually post your image at the scheduled time you selected. Instead, it will send you a reminder at that time to post it.

The great thing about this is that outside of the actual image; you can easily copy and paste the rest of the information. This saves you a ton of time in trying to think of the perfect description.

Personally, I'd advise you to start working on a week's worth of content from the start. If you plan on posting twice per day, your calendar should have at least 14 pieces of content. If you post 3 times per day, you should have 21 pieces of content.

But how do you know what content to post? What's going to be popular with your audience?

Remember before we created your profile, I told you to research the top influencers in your niche? Well, it's time to use that knowledge.

Go back to their profiles and take another look at their content. Pay special attention to the top six posts because that is their latest ones.

What do you notice about their photos? Their videos?

More importantly, how's the engagement on those posts?

Now there's a lot of different kinds of content that's popular depending on your chosen niche.

For some, high-quality photos are the most important posts you can do. For others, a video is the best.

My opinion, a mix of photos and videos are very important. The photos draw in immediate attention, and the videos provide great information or entertainment.

In the next section, I'll show you how to create attention-grabbing content like an influencer.

How to Create Content Like an Influencer

Here's a social media tip that everyone should know. Video always performs better than photos.

It's better for social media posts, entertainment, and advertisements.

If you don't believe me? Ask your friends what they rather look at. A photo of a new phone that's about to be released, or a video highlighting the new features of the phone? I'm pretty sure the video will be the popular choice.

At the same time, Instagram is known as a platform to post great photos, so you want to add some greats pictures as well as videos.

My rule of thumb is 1 photo and 1 video posted per day. If you're posting 3 times per day, make that 2 photos and 1 video per day.

"But I thought you said videos were better than photos?"

I did say that, but too much of a good thing gets boring. Think of your videos as a nice treat to compliment your photos.

Now that you have your content ready to go, we need to make a few tweaks to make it stand out.

Unless you are a professional photographer, videographer, or you're curating content from one of them, your content isn't going to be perfect from the start.

But there are features and applications to make your photos and videos stand out from the crowd.

The two things I always use for my content are Instagram's filters and an app called Inshot.

Everyone knows about Instagram's filters. They can make anyone look like supermodels and make areas look stunning. That's why when you post an image, you should go through all of the filters that they offer.

You don't have to use any of the filters. They may look worse on your photo than if you just leave it alone. But give the filters a look and see if they will make your photo pop out more. If it seems amazing to you, it will to someone else as well.

My other suggestion is that you download the app Inshot. Inshot is a photo and video editing application that allows you to add emojis, text, and much more to your content.

I personally use this for all of my videos and use a specific technique that I learned from an Instagram influencer named Thor Aarsand.

When you post a video on Instagram, it allows you to choose a specific frame of the video to be the thumbnail (the same way YouTube does). You can take advantage of this through Inshot.

Open the app and select the video button. From there you are going to choose your video and trim it so that it is no more than 1 minute long.

Go through your video and find the best shot that can grab someone's attention.

For example, if you post a funny video of someone falling, you can use the frame that shows the person falling backward as your thumbnail.

Next, you are going to go to the text section and simply write the letter "O" in red.

You're going to use this O as a circle to highlight the best part of your video. It'll instantly grab someone's attention and increase the number of video views you'll get.

If the O seems too thick to be a circle, you can simply change the font so that it looks thinner (something that took me 8 videos to figure out).

After you drag your new circle over to the part of the video that captures viewers attention, you have to adjust how long that circle stays there.

It won't just be on the thumbnail, but it will be in the actual video as well. You want to shorten the length to where it shows up where your thumbnail frame is and instantly disappears.

If you want to make your video stand out more, you can also add stickers.

I tend to use the devil emoji sticker or the eyes and keep them throughout the entire video.

After that, you can save the video in 1080p and instantly share it on Instagram.

If you need a video tutorial on this, you can check out Thor's video on Inshot right over HERE.

If you stick with these small changes, and you keep your content based on your niche passion, you will be a master content creator.

But what if you're not creating content? What if you are reposting viral content on your page?

Don't worry; I got you covered on that too.

How to Find Awesome Content to "Steal"

Did you ever hear one of Steve Job's most controversial statements regarding innovation?

It went something like this.

"Good artists copy, great artists steal."

I am about to turn you into a great artist.

Before I get into how to find awesome photos and videos that you can repost on your page. You have to remember one rule of courtesy.

Always credit the owner

If you were a content creator, you would hate to see someone who posted your work and claimed it for their own right?

Well, same goes for other people if you post their photos and videos without crediting them. It does not take much more work to give them the credit they deserve.

In the very least you can write their Instagram handle in the description of the photo. Let your followers know that this is the original creator of this work.

Whenever I'm curating content, I do this and tag them in the actual photo or video. It establishes credibility and trust with both the creator and my followers, which will be good in case you decide to curate more work from that creator.

Now it's time to find awesome, viral content to post on your Instagram.

The first thing to do is find an Instagram account in the same niche as you that has over 100,000 followers.

Skip over the first 3 images and count the total number of likes and comments on the next 10.

Take the total amount of likes and comments. Divide those number by 10, then multiply that number by 1.5. This gives you the number of likes and comments you're looking for on their page.

Now find some images that have more likes and more comments than this number. These are the photos and videos that are viral.

If you manage to do this with 5 different accounts, find 2 pieces of content on each page, and do this 3 times. You'll have enough content to last a month. Now that's working smarter.

That works every time for photos, but what about videos? You can't just simply screenshot a video or download it from Instagram.

Or can you?

There's an impressive app that allows you to download videos right from Instagram. Easy enough, it's called Video Downloader. It looks just like the Instagram app and here's a photo to show you.

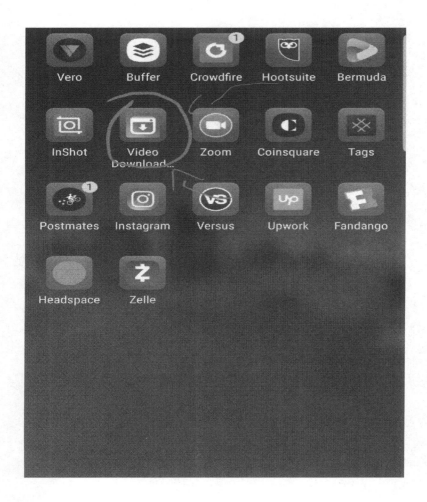

It's really easy to use.

First, find a video on Instagram that you want to download.

On the top right you'll see three dots that represent the settings for that post.

Tap the option to copy the link, and Video Downloader should pop up. If not, open the app and paste the link.

The video should be downloaded onto your smartphone.

Now you can take this video, put it on Inshot to make your thumbnail and schedule it on Buffer to post on your Instagram.

Three days worth of work turned into a month's worth of viral content for you.

Now that we've discussed the different types of content you can post on your Instagram account, and how to effectively post them. We are going to dive deeper into posting images and making them the best they can be.

Action Steps

1) **Create a content calendar and keep at least 2 weeks worth of content scheduled.**

2) **Research the type of content your audience likes and create similar posts for your profile.**

3) **Research and find viral content to curate on your page. Use Inshot to create thumbnails for your videos.**

CHAPTER 6: TREAT YOUR INSTAGRAM STORIES LIKE A VLOG.

Snapchat had a chance to be a real monster in social media.

Their visual messaging app that let you send photos and videos as stories that disappear after a certain amount of time was really popular with teens and young adults.

Then they got an offer to be bought out from Facebook and rejected it.

One thing you don't want to do is reject Mark Zuckerberg; it may just come back to haunt you. Since Facebook owns Instagram, they decided to have their own stories feature to compete with Snapchat.

Boy did they ever beat Snapchat?

Currently, many Snapchat users are switching over to Instagram stories, and Snapchat stocks are plummeting.

But what does this have to do with you and your page?

Snapchats loss is your gain.

With Instagram stories, you can form a deeper relationship with your followers than just having them like your posts.

You can choose to bring them into your life and connect with them.

Which is what I'm going to show you how to do in this chapter

I'm going to teach you how to form that connection with your followers on Instagram using stories. You'll also know how many stories you should be posting daily and what features you should take advantage of.

How to Use Instagram Stories To Connect With Your Followers

Posts and stories are two entirely different strategies.

With posts, I told you to focus on the quality of your posts. That it had to go along with your niche, your passion, and that it had to look as perfect as possible.

Throw that all away when it comes to stories.

You should use Instagram stories to show the behind the scenes life of the person behind the camera.

Show your followers what you do on a daily basis.

We all have lives outside of social media. Some of us are students trying to get the best grades that we can to graduate. Some of us work 1 or more jobs to pay our bills or to establish a career.

Some of us do both

Let your followers see what you do. It doesn't have to be entertaining, just has to be genuine.

Take Vloggers on YouTube for example. One of my favorite vlogging channels is Nikki and John Vlogs.

Do they have top-notch production skills...no

Do they work to make me laugh every 5 minutes....not on this channel at least?

But I still watch them every day they post. Why?

Because I am invested in their lives that they brought me in.

Through their vlogs, I got to see their engagement, the birth of their daughter, and their move from California back to Minnesota.

I felt like I was a part of their family because they brought us all into it.

That's what you have to do for your followers with stories.

Bring them into your lives. Bring them into the happiest moments so they can cheer beside you.

If you're comfortable with it, bring them into the struggles and things that don't always go right. Let them see that you do have struggles and you are also a person like them.

Let them see the daily grind of what you're doing. Whether that's climbing the corporate ladder at your job, establishing a business, or being a creator online.

If you're honest with your followers about who you are, they will love and feel connected with you more than they do with your content.

How Many Stories Should You Be Posting?

A good number of posts on Instagram is around 2-3 per day. For stories, it should be double.

You want to have 4-6 story posts per day to show your followers what you are doing on a daily basis.

Does it sound harder than creating 2-3 regular posts?

It's really not.

This is how you create a story on Instagram.

1) On your Instagram feed in the home page, tap on the camera button on the top left corner.
2) Take your photo or video.
3) Click on the add to story on the bottom of the screen.

Done, you just finished creating a story in about 1 minute.

Can you make around 4-6 of those per day?

I believe you can.

In fact, I think you can do close to 10 of those per day, but let's not get too carried away with ourselves.

There's still need to be some sort of quality in these stories.

Treat it the same way YouTubers treat vlogs.

Use it to record what you're doing at the moment and during the day.

If you're just waking up, take a selfie in bed saying good morning.

If you're at work, take a photo from inside the breakroom.

Going out to eat? Take a video of the vibe from inside the restaurant.

People want to live vicariously through others. Let them want to live through you.

The Best Features In Instagram Stories

This part will be really short.

I want to show you my favorite features in Instagram stories that I pretty much use each week.

When you record a video or photo for stories, you'll see this little smiley face on the top right that has a bunch of stickers you can use. In that stickers section, there are two that I absolutely love using. The hashtag and polls.

Remember earlier when we were creating your account, I said you wanted to create a hashtag so people can follow it.

Here's where that comes in handy.

On top of showing posts when people follow hashtags, they can also see stories that use the hashtag.

Put your hashtag somewhere in the story so that your followers (and other users) can see your story.

Polls are my absolute favorite way to talk to my followers.

On my gaming page, I put a poll on Instagram stories to see what video games my followers want me to play.

You can only have two options, so I'll put two video games that I enjoy playing and let them vote.

Don't go crazy like I used to and checked every 5 minutes. Post it up and don't check it until you are about to go to bed. Let your followers get the chance to see it and cast their vote.

This will help you connect more with your followers because you can pretty much ask them anything and get their opinions.

Do not neglect these steps. If you want to build a community of people around you and your content, utilize stories and these features.

It also helps you out with Instagram's algorithm. They love users who use all of their features.

Action Steps

1) **Start using Instagram Stories to bring your followers into your life.**
2) **Post at least 4-6 stories per day.**
3) **Utilize stickers, polls, and hashtags to make your stories more interesting and pop with Instagram.**

CHAPTER 7:
#HASHTAGS: THE BEST WAY TO GET EXPOSURE WHEN YOU'RE STARTING OUT.

So you have your audience, you created your profile, have your content scheduled and ready to go, and have some stories so people can know you.

Now it's time to get your name out there and maximize your followers.

The best way to gain exposure for your Instagram account when you are first starting out is through <u>RELATABLE</u> and <u>RESEARCHED</u> hashtags.

People use hashtags all the time when they post content on social media. But the same amount of people also search through hashtags to find content.

In this chapter, I'll show you how to effectively find and utilize the right hashtags to gain exposure and followers to your page. You will also learn how many hashtags to put on each page and where to put them.

Now it's time to be discovered.

How To Research Hashtags to Gain Maximum Exposure.

Believe it or not.

Instagram is the best place to research hashtags on Instagram (duh).

Instagram allows you to search hashtags and see just how many posts utilize this hashtag.

The best part of searching hashtags on Instagram is that Instagram will also suggest more hashtags that others search for.

Take note on these for later.

Write down every hashtag related to your content that has at least 100,000 posts.

We're going to use these when we incorporate it to your posts.

While Instagram is the best place to find hashtags to use on your posts, it isn't the only way.

There are other great ways to research hashtags that will find more than what you even thought of.

One app that I started using is called Tags.

Tags is an Android and IOS app that allows you to upload a photo and automatically generates 30 hashtags that Tags think are related to the photo.

While you have to judge whether or not these hashtags are related to your content, it's a good place to check for tags that you may not have thought about.

Now you should have a nice list of hashtags that you can use to grow your exposure.

Remember to write these down because we are going to use them right now.

How Many Hashtags Should You Put on Your Posts?

Now I don't know the perfect number of hashtags you should be posting.

Different influencers and managers will give you different numbers.

Some people think 30 hashtags is the perfect number because using the maximum number of hashtags is supposed to give you maximum exposure.

Some people believe 10 hashtags are best because the algorithm does not like using a lot of hashtags.

My personal opinion, both of these numbers are correct.

Having 10 hashtags is a good number for exposure and making your posts look clean.

At the same time, Instagram does not like users using the same hashtags for multiple posts in a day.

That's when the 30 hashtags come into play.

Hopefully, your hashtag research led you to have a list of at least 30 tags along with the number of posts.

Now we need to organize them.

Break up the hashtags into three groups.

   1) Tags that have between 100,000-200,000 posts.
   2) Tags that have between 300,000-600,000 posts.

3) Tags that have over 600,000 posts.

There are reasons for this organization.

The ultimate goal is to have your content ranked for these hashtags.

When I say rank, I mean having your photos and videos show up in the top 6 results when someone searches up the hashtag.

If you can get on the top 6, that pretty much guarantees that more people will see your content and engage on it.

Your strategy is to take our three hashtag groups and create three mixed groups of hashtags that you cycle through for each post.

Each group will include the following.

1) 4 hashtags in the 100,000 - 200,000 group.
2) 3 hashtags in the 300,000 - 600,000 group.
3) 3 hashtags in the 600,000 - 1,000,000 group.

Why do we do this? Because we are looking for a domino effect to take place.

Let's say you post one photo. The engagement from your following will allow you to rank in the 100,000 - 200,000 group.

Once you rank in that group, the extra attention and engagement you will receive will bump you up to rank in the 300,000 - 600,000 group.

Over time, your follower's engagement along with these bumps will allow you to rank in 600,000 - 1,000,000 group.

You continue to do this over and over; you can begin to expand your hashtags specifically to competitive hashtags that have over 1,000,000 posts.

Use these groups to maximize the amount of exposure without Instagram thinking that you are a spammer and you will start seeing more likes and followers on your content.

Where To Place Hashtags On Your Posts

Another question that many people cannot answer about Instagram.

Where are we supposed to put the hashtags?

Some people put their hashtags in the description of their content, and others think the comments are the best place.

Again, the answer is both.

Put 3 comments in the description of your post and the rest as the first comment. It keeps your post looking clean yet has the same effect with the hashtags.

Action Steps

1) **Organize your hashtags in 3 groups**

2) **Mix your hashtags into 3 groups of 10**

3) **Place 3 hashtags in the description and the rest as the first comment**

CHAPTER 8:
YOU NEED TO ENGAGE WITH EVERYONE.

Yes; the name of this chapter is accurate.

For others to find and engage with your content, you also need to engage with other people's content.

You are not some big shot who can receive without giving.

In this chapter, you are going to learn how to get users to engage with your content.

You are also going to learn how to engage with others content and how to automate the process entirely.

You need to show others that you are 100% active on Instagram, then engagement is the biggest way.

How to Get Users To Engage on your Content

Engagement is the biggest way to show Instagram that people love your posts. Every like and comment tells Instagram that you are awesome.

To get this engagement, you need to post consistently and post quality content.

The consistency shows users that your Instagram account is active and they'll receive value. The quality shows that you care about the things you post.

You focus on these two things; your followers will show their appreciation through engagements.

But the one engagement you are really looking for is their comments.

Comments mean more than likes because it shows that your followers actually took the time and cared about your content.

Anyone can press a button. Real engagement comes through the comments section. Remember that.

With that said, there is a big no-no when it comes to likes and comments.

Never buy them.

There's a ton of websites that allow you to buy likes, comments, and even followers for your account and content.

It's best to stay far away from these services because they always end in 1 of 3 ways.

1) It's a scam site that doesn't give you the engagement that you paid for.
2) It leaves you with engagement from ghost accounts that will never engage with your other content.
3) If Instagram finds out about you buying engagement; they terminate your account.

I don't want you to deal with any of these possibilities, so it's best to earn the engagement of others.

Do Unto Others as You Want Done to You.

Remember, you're not a big shot yet. You can't expect to receive a ton of engagement from people without having to engage with them.

Outside of "like for like," "comment for comment," or "follow for follow" situations, you absolutely need to engage with your community and others who share in the same passions as you do.

You need to do this a lot.

But who should you be engaging with and how much engagement should you do?

The answer...targeted people and a lot.

By targeted people, I am talking about the ones we have been studying and looking for pretty much in this entire book. Just search one of the hashtags on your list. Under the top results should be another section called "recent." This is where you engage with others.

People who post will always check notifications on their most recent content. It's one of those things that make humans vain; we love when people love us.

So if you go through your list, like and comment on as much recent content as you can, that's more eyes that are seeing your profile.

But I know that seems very general, and we need an exact number of people to engage with. Thankfully, Gary Vaynerchuk has a number for us.

Gary Vee himself came up with an impressive strategy known as the $1.80 strategy.

Essentially, if you comment (or give you 2 cents) to 90 people each day, you'll grow on social media.

So I'll tell you to break this up into chunks. Take 9 hashtags from your list, and comment on the 10 most recent pictures from each hashtag.

There is your $1.80 strategy.

But what if you're too busy for this? What if you can't possibly comment on this many profiles because you have classes, work, kids, and a ton of other responsibilities.

Don't worry; we have something for that as well. It's called automation.

How To Automate Your Instagram Account to Engage In Your Sleep

This is one area that people find morally wrong in social media. People who automate their accounts to engage with other people's profiles 24/7.

Many people find this wrong because the likes and comments are not genuine from the owner of the account. They are absolutely right.

But we're not doing this to be genuine; we are doing this to maximize our amount of engagement and exposure while living our regular lives.

If you absolutely do not want to automate your Instagram account and believe you can do this manually, I say go for it. I've done it previously, and it is possible.

But automation does it a lot faster, which is one aspect we all want.

You'll find a lot of automation services, but there's one that I use that has given me great results.

This service is called FollowU, and it is entirely brand new as of the time I'm writing this book.

FollowU is an amazing automation tool that allows you to target certain Instagram profiles and content based on the accounts they follow, number of followers, number of likes and comments on their content, and so much more. It even spaces out the amount of engagement, so it looks as if a real person is doing it.

The best part is that it's really not expensive to automate your profile through FollowU. It costs $35/month to automate one account and $45/month for a boosted version of this. The boost means your engagement happens more frequent. They also have more expensive plans that let you automate up to 6 accounts, but you're not ready for this...yet.

Personally, I go with the boosted account. You get faster engagement for only $10 more, plus it can lead you to make money on Instagram, which means it's a small investment and a tax write off.

Action Steps

1) **Post consistently to get followers engaging on your posts**
2) **Use Gary Vaynerchuk's $1.80 strategy to engage with others.**
3) **Bonus: Use FollowU to automate your engagements.**

CHAPTER 9: HOW TO GET PAID TO SHOUTOUT PEOPLE AND BRANDS.

I know for many of you, this is the chapter you've been waiting for. But there's a reason that I saved this chapter for last.

Making money off Instagram should be the last thing you think of.

My goal for Instagram is to build a community of people who shared the same passions that I did, and that should be your goal as well.

But if you put in the time, got to know your followers and post consistent quality content, you deserve this last chapter.

Here I am also going to show you how to get paid through shoutouts and brand deals.

I am also going to show you how to drive your followers onto your website. Whether it's your store, appointment calendar, or to more online content.

This is the final step to becoming an Instagram influencer and a master of the platform.

Getting Paid to Shout Out Other Users and Brands

You would not believe how incredibly easy this is. When you start growing on Instagram, believe me, people will notice and start messaging you for shoutouts.

People will comment on your photos, hit you in the DMs, and do whatever they can to get you to check out their stuff.

I had just reached 200 followers on my gaming page when I started getting messages from other gamers to shout them out on Instagram, follow them on Twitch, or check out their YouTube channels. Check out these photos.

I'd advise not to start taking payments for shoutouts and brand deals until you have at least 10,000 followers. If you do take payments before then, your followers may see you as a sellout.

I care about my following and what they think of me, so I still haven't taken a single dime to shoutout anyone.

But when the time does come to monetize your account, you need to know your worth. How much are you going to charge for these shoutouts?

This number is crucial because if you charge too little, then you undervalued the power of your account. You charge too much; now you overvalued yourself to both this person and anyone after.

Don't worry; I know an awesome (and free) way to check how much your shout outs are worth. It's called the Instagram Money Calculator.

Influencer Marketing Hub has this awesome calculator that checks the number of followers and engagement rate that you have on your profile. It takes this number and comes up with a range that you can charge for a shoutout.

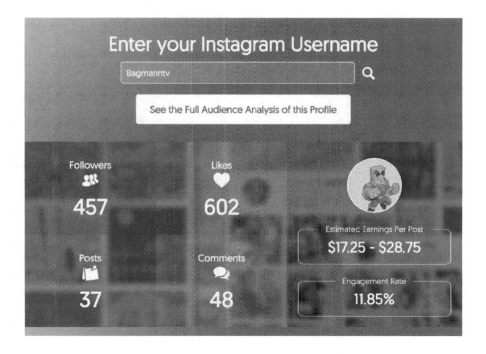

This is why I said that engagement was so important, the higher your engagement rate, the more you can charge for a shoutout.

I would charge the higher end of the range if I were willing to do a shoutout. If they accepted it, that's awesome. If they didn't, it gives you more wiggle room in negotiation. Even if you accept a lower payment, you'll still be making money that matches your value.

The same strategy can be tweaks slightly for brand deals. You can message brands and offer to do a shoutout for them for a certain price, or they can hit you up with an offer.

Many brands offer one of three options for deals.

1) They pay you upfront for a shoutout on your page.

2) They offer you a percentage of the revenue generated after you post your shoutout

3) They offer you free merchandise in exchange for a shoutout.

I actually organized this in order from best to worst scenarios.

Getting paid upfront is the best for shoutouts because you know you will get paid for your shoutout, even if the product is a complete dud. You should always leverage the power of your account and try to negotiate this type of deal.

A percentage based deal is okay, but only if you're confident that people will actually go to the brand's site and buy. If they don't, then the brand just got free publicity, and you got nothing to show for it. If a company offers this kind of deal, try to negotiate them to an upfront deal.

The free merchandise I will only recommend if the brand is new or very small. If they're a clothing company, designing their stuff out of a basement, then I would consider the merchandise deal. It does give you some free stuff along with the chance to build a relationship with the brand. Who knows, maybe they'll blow up, and you can become the face of the brand.

When you listen to an offer from a brand, be sure to do your research on how big they are. If they are a well-known, big name brand, they will have the money to pay you upfront. If they are that small brand that has absolutely nothing, then take the merchandise and build on that relationship.

Driving Traffic From Instagram To Your Website

This is my favorite thing to do. Driving my followers from Instagram to my Twitch channel means a lot to me. It proves that I do have a following that is there for me.

That's what building a community is all about. You have your community too, so it's time to drive them to your website.

Remember when you put that website in your bio? Well, we're going to be taking advantage of it finally.

You are going to use the power of your content to tell people to click on that link. It's going to take everything you've learned to make it happen.

We're going to keep this short and sweet.

1) Create an awesome photo or video about your online content, store, or service provided.
2) Provide a call to action in the video or description telling your followers to click the link in your bio

Done.

It is literally that simple, but it is not easy.

You'll have to understand that not many people will click on your link right away. They may still be trying to get used to you and the content you put on Instagram before they trust you enough to click on a link that takes them somewhere else.

That's okay, just keep posting great content on Instagram and eventually they will trust you more.

If you want to blend this strategy along with brand deals, a bonus tip is to use Bitly.com or Google Analytics to measure the number of clicks your link gets.

You can take the number of clicks to brands and people who want a shoutout from you. This adds more leverage when you negotiate on how much to charge.

You see how everything you've learned in this book has just come together effortlessly.

Action Steps

1)   **Wait until you reach 10,000 followers before monetizing Instagram page.**

2)   **Know how much your page is worth before determining a price for shoutouts.**

3)   **Always go for an upfront payment from brands.**

Conclusion

Well, congratulations!

You are officially an expert on Instagram and on your way to influencer status.

You really should give yourself a pat on the back, you survived this whole book, my ramblings, and hopefully took the steps needed to build your name and brand.

But remember what I said in the very beginning.

The tricky thing about social media is that it is constantly changing. Many of the tips I gave you now may not work 5 years down the road.

While I'll be updating this book to go along with the many changes Instagram will make, I want to make sure that you are getting the necessary advice and tips to continue to grow your social media right away.

That's why I am offering you the chance to join my email list and be up to date on monthly changes that may take place on Instagram.

Don't worry; you won't get any unnecessary spam from me. Nothing but valuable information that will help you on your journey to becoming an influencer.

If you don't want any emails and can wait for the revised version of this book, that's awesome.

But if you want to always be up to date so you can beat the competition before they ever find out, just go to:

https://mailchi.mp/74d02e4344d5/master-social-media

Either way, I wish you nothing but the best on your influencer journey.